The Gift of Tongues

An Examination of What the Bible Teaches
Concerning the Spiritual Gift of Tongues

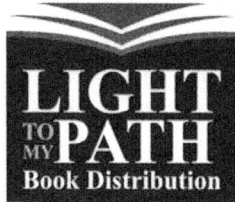

F. Wayne Mac Leod

Light To My Path Book Distribution
Sydney Mines, Nova Scotia, CANADA

Table of Contents

Preface

"And they were all filled with the Holy Spirit and began to speak in other tongues as the Spirit gave them utterance." (Acts 2:4)

This is one of a variety of passages in the Bible about what has become known as the gift of tongues. It is a controversial practice in the church of our day and one that has become a source of deep theological divisions. Believers have taken different sides in this debate, and the result has often been an imbalanced understanding of what the Bible teaches.

On the one extreme, we have churches demanding that all who believe in Jesus and are filled with His Spirit speak in tongues. This requirement has produced a whole crop of pretenders who claim to speak in tongues, but the language they speak is not from the Spirit.

On the other hand, we have churches insisting that this gift is no longer relevant. In the churches that I have frequented, I have yet to hear a message or teaching on this gift of God to the early church! This has led to ignorance of the gift and its purpose in the unfolding of God's plan.

Listen to Paul's counsel to Timothy in 2 Timothy 3:

[16] All Scripture is breathed out by God and profitable for teaching, for reproof, for correction, and for training in righteousness, [17] that the man of God may be complete, equipped for every good work. (2 Timothy 3)

To those who ignore the teaching of Scripture on the gift of tongues, I bring this challenge. The fact that Acts 2:4 and others like it are found in the Bible, implies that the gift is significant in God's purpose for the church and should not be ignored.

To those who promote this gift, I bring this challenge. It is crucial that every gift of God be used as He intends. All gifts of the Spirit are subject to the principles of Scripture. In other words, a gift of God can be misused. If we want to use the gifts God gives as He intends, we must carefully examine the teaching of Scripture and submit to God's purpose for the use of these gifts. God's gifts must be used in God's way.

In this study, it is my purpose to examine the teaching of Scripture about the gift of tongues and the purpose of God for its use. I trust it will be a blessing and promote a greater understanding and unity among the people of God.

God bless,

F. Wayne Mac Leod

CHAPTER 1 -
The Confusion of Language

I want to begin this study with an examination of Genesis 9 and 11. Let me put this in context. God created Adam and Eve and placed them on the Garden of Eden. It wasn't long before they fell into sin and rebellion against God. Sin increased in the world through their descendants to a point where Genesis 6 tells us:

[5] The LORD saw that the wickedness of man was great in the earth, and that every intention of the thoughts of his heart was only evil continually. [6] And the LORD regretted that he had made man on the earth, and it grieved him to his heart. [7] So the LORD said, "I will blot out man whom I have created from the face of the land, man and animals and creeping things and birds of the heavens, for I am sorry that I have made them." (Genesis 6)

The human race came under the wrath of its Creator. God determined in His heart that He would destroy the world as it was known. He sent a great flood to destroy all living beings apart from Noah, his family and the animals they took on the ark. We read about this in Genesis 6-8.

After the destruction of all life, God released Noah and his family from the ark. In Genesis 9, God spoke to Noah and his descendants:

[9:1] And God blessed Noah and his sons and said to them, "Be fruitful and multiply and fill the earth. [2] The

fear of you and the dread of you shall be upon every beast of the earth and upon every bird of the heavens, upon everything that creeps on the ground and all the fish of the sea. Into your hand they are delivered. [3] Every moving thing that lives shall be food for you. And as I gave you the green plants, I give you everything. [4] But you shall not eat flesh with its life, that is, its blood. [5] And for your lifeblood I will require a reckoning: from every beast I will require it and from man. From his fellow man I will require a reckoning for the life of man.

> *[6] "Whoever sheds the blood of man,*
> *by man shall his blood be shed,*
> *for God made man in his own image.*

[7] And you, be fruitful and multiply, increase greatly on the earth and multiply in it." [8] Then God said to Noah and to his sons with him, [9] "Behold, I establish my covenant with you and your offspring after you, [10] and with every living creature that is with you, the birds, the livestock, and every beast of the earth with you, as many as came out of the ark; it is for every beast of the earth. [11] I establish my covenant with you, that never again shall all flesh be cut off by the waters of the flood, and never again shall there be a flood to destroy the earth." (Genesis 9)

Notice what God told Noah and his family in this passage.

God Reveals His Purpose

First, God revealed His purpose for Noah and his descendants. He states this purpose twice here.

"Be fruitful and multiply and fill the earth" (verse 1).

"And you, be fruitful and multiply, increase greatly on the earth and multiply in it" (verse 7)

God intended that the survivors of the flood "fill the earth" and "increase greatly." In other words, they were to spread out over the surface of the land, have children and form nations.

God Entrusted Them with His Authority

Notice second that God gave these men and women authority and dominion over the earth.

[2] The fear of you and the dread of you shall be upon every beast of the earth and upon every bird of the heavens, upon everything that creeps on the ground and all the fish of the sea. Into your hand they are delivered. [3] Every moving thing that lives shall be food for you. And as I gave you the green plants, I give you everything. (Genesis 9)

As the survivors of the flood spread out over the earth, they would go with the authority of God. They were to rule over the earth and to use its resources for food and shelter. They would lack nothing to accomplish their God-given mandate of filling the earth.

God Entered a Covenant with Them

Notice also from these verses that God entered a covenant with the survivors of the flood.

[9] "Behold, I establish my covenant with you and your offspring after you, [10] and with every living creature that is with you, the birds, the livestock, and every beast of the earth with you, as many as came out of the ark; it is

for every beast of the earth. [11] I establish my covenant with you, that never again shall all flesh be cut off by the waters of the flood, and never again shall there be a flood to destroy the earth." (Genesis 9)

The covenant that God made was a covenant of mercy. He promised that His favour would be on them as they fulfilled His purpose for the earth. He would protect them and grant them His special mercy. He told them that He would never again destroy all flesh as He had done. They had the promise of God's mercy and blessing as they repopulated and spread out over the surface of the land.

God Placed Them Under and Obligation of Obedience

Finally, God placed humanity under an obligation of obedience. Notice what He told them in verse 4:

[4] But you shall not eat flesh with its life, that is, its blood. (Genesis 9)

Blood belonged to God. By extension, their lives belonged to God. Whoever shed the blood of another human being would be punished by death. All human beings belonged to God. They were to respect His Lordship and walk in obedience to Him.

Genesis 9 tells us that God called the survivors of the flood to fill the earth and have dominion over it. They were to do so as those who had entered a covenant relationship with God. The seriousness of this obligation was obvious to those who had just recently experienced the devastation of the flood because of rebellion against God.

It is in the context of God's command to His people that we must now examine Genesis 11. We discover from verse 1 that the whole earth had one language:

10

[1] Now the whole earth had one language and the same words. (Genesis 11)

As these survivors of the flood moved eastward, they came to the region of Shinar and settled there. They seemed to enjoy this region and decided that they would remain there and build a permanent city. Notice the reason for building a permanent city:

[4] Then they said, "Come, let us build ourselves a city and a tower with its top in the heavens, and let us make a name for ourselves, lest we be dispersed over the face of the whole earth."

According to Genesis 11:4, they did not want to be "dispersed over the face of the whole earth." They grew comfortable with each other and felt that their greatness would be found in remaining together. What is vital for us to understand is that this was contrary to the command of God. God told them to fill the earth. Obedience to this command required that they disperse over the face of the whole earth. This was precisely what they did not want to do. By settling in Shinar, they were purposefully disobeying God and His purpose for them. This act of disobedience brought the wrath of God upon them:

[5] And the LORD came down to see the city and the tower, which the children of man had built. [6] And the LORD said, "Behold, they are one people, and they have all one language, and this is only the beginning of what they will do. And nothing that they propose to do will now be impossible for them. [7] Come, let us go down and there confuse their language, so that they may not understand one another's speech." [8] So the LORD dispersed them from there over the face of all the earth, and they left off building the city. [9] Therefor, its name was called Babel, because there the LORD confused the

11

*language of all the earth. And from there the LORD
dispersed them over the face of all the earth. (Genesis
11)*

Notice what happened in these verses. The people chose to remain together rather than fulfil the mandate of God. They could remain together because they spoke the same language and understood each other. God chose to confuse their language, so they would not understand each other's speech.

While we do not know the specific details of what took place that day, what is clear is that one moment the people were speaking together and understanding each other and the next they were speaking in words their neighbour did not understand. The result was that they were "dispersed over the face of all the earth" (Genesis 11:9). This was God's purpose from the beginning. He wanted to populate the entire earth, and when the survivors of the flood refused to do so, he confused their language and forced them into obedience.

God chose ordinary people who had learned a specific language from their youth and gave them another speech. Understand here that this new language was not a learned language. The context indicates that it was miraculously given to them by God. Nor was it a language that already existed on the earth. Genesis 11:1 makes this abundantly clear:

*[1] Now the whole earth had one language and the same
words. (Genesis 11)*

These people began to speak with words they had never spoken before. They formed sentences and communicated in this new language. It appears from the context that different languages were given to them by

God and those who were given a similar tongue grouped together and left the region to settle elsewhere.

This was a work of God. It was an amazing work. God gave groups of people a whole new set of words and the ability to communicate in those words. The imparting of these new tongues seemed to be instantaneous. We can only imagine the confusion there would have been in those days as people unsuccessfully tried to communicate with their friends.

We will read nothing more in Scripture about this miraculous gift until we come to the book of Acts. There on the day of Pentecost, the Spirit of God fell on the believers who had gathered together in one place. Listen to the record of what transpired that day:

[2:1] When the day of Pentecost arrived, they were all together in one place. [2] And suddenly there came from heaven a sound like a mighty rushing wind, and it filled the entire house where they were sitting. [3] And divided tongues as of fire appeared to them and rested on each one of them. [4] And they were all filled with the Holy Spirit and began to speak in other tongues as the Spirit gave them utterance. (Acts 2)

The Spirit of God fell on this group of believers and gave them the ability to speak in other tongues. We will talk about this more fully in the next chapter but what is clear is that foreigners in Jerusalem that day identified the languages the believers spoke as common languages of the day (Acts 2:7-11).

In Genesis 11, we see the formation of different language groups and nations. We also see how God set His heart on the descendants of Noah through Shem and Abraham. These would be His people. God, however, also had a purpose for the rest of the nations and language groups. In Acts 2, we see how He began the process of restoring these foreign nations to Himself. Through the work of the Lord Jesus, Gentile nations would be brought to God. In Genesis 11, God separated these nations by the confusion of tongues. Now in Acts 2, He gave a similar gift and brought them back to Himself. People from many nations, gathered in Jerusalem on the day of Pentecost heard the gospel of Jesus Christ for the first time through the miraculous gift of tongues given to the believers that day. God was revealing to those present that He also had a purpose for the nations He had scattered from Shinar after the flood.

CHAPTER 2 -
The Languages of Pentecost

Many years passed since different languages were given at the Tower of Babel. Jesus came to the earth and, by His death, opened the way for foreigners to become children of God. It was now the day of Pentecost, and Christians had gathered together in one place (Acts 2:1). Something wonderful happened in that assembly of believers. Without warning, they heard a sound from heaven. It was like a rushing wind filling the place where they were sitting (Acts 2:2). Those present listened to this sound and wondered what it was.

What was peculiar about this wind was that it visibly divided into what those believers described as "tongues of fire." These tongues separated and rested on each one present. When they rested on them, they began to speak another language as the Spirit enabled them.

[3] And divided tongues as of fire appeared to them and rested on each one of them. [4] And they were all filled with the Holy Spirit and began to speak in other tongues as the Spirit gave them utterance. (Acts 2)

We need to notice several details in these verses.

Notice first that the believers saw something that day. They described what they saw as "tongues." The use of this word is quite peculiar. The Greek word used is "glossa," which refers to the organ of the body. What they saw was identified as the human organ used to produce sound and speech. The tongues they saw appeared to be of fire. It would have been more natural for these believers to speak of a flame of fire, but they all describe what they saw as tongues.

Notice second that the word "tongues" is plural. There was not one single tongue but many tongues of fire that came to rest on the individuals present. When that tongue rested on an individual, he or she would begin to speak in what is described in verse 4 as "other tongues" or other languages. There was not one single language spoken, but many.

The final detail I would like to mention from verses 3-4 is the fact that these believers began to speak other languages, "as the Spirit gave them utterance." In other words, the language they spoke was given to them by the Holy Spirit. Like is was in the days of Noah's descendants, these believers began to communicate in a language they did not previously know. The ability to speak this foreign language was a miraculous and instantaneous gift from the Spirit. Without prior study or knowledge of this language, the believers spoke clearly in that tongue.

We find evidence of this in verses 5-6. The inhabitants of Jerusalem heard the commotion that took place when these believers began to speak. They came rushing to the place where they were and listened to what they were saying. To their surprise, they heard these early Christians speak in known languages of the day.

[5] Now there were dwelling in Jerusalem Jews, devout men from every nation under heaven. [6] And at this sound the multitude came together, and they were bewildered, because each one was hearing them speak in his own language. [7] And they were amazed and

astonished, saying, "Are not all these who are speaking Galileans? [8] And how is it that we hear, each of us in his own native language? [9] Parthians and Medes and Elamites and residents of Mesopotamia, Judea and Cappadocia, Pontus and Asia, [10] Phrygia and Pamphylia, Egypt and the parts of Libya belonging to Cyrene, and visitors from Rome, [11] both Jews and proselytes, Cretans and Arabians—we hear them telling in our own tongues the mighty works of God." (Acts 2)

The inhabitants of Jerusalem identified the languages spoken that day. People of many nations heard about the "mighty works of God" (verse 11), in their language. The good news about Jesus Christ was now declared to those who were separated from God's people in the days of Noah. Through the gift of tongues, God had separated the nations from His people after the flood. Now, through the gift of tongues, those same nations were being called back. God had not forsaken them forever. He had a purpose for these Gentile nations as well.

The context indicates that the believers made quite a noise. Verse 6 tells us that "at this sound, the multitude came together." The response of the crowd to what they heard is described in verses 5-13. They were "bewildered" in verse 5. Verse 7 tells us that they were "amazed and astonished." Verse 12 tells us that the crowd was "amazed and perplexed." Not all those who heard the believers that day responded positively—some mocked them and accused them of being drunk (verse 13).

To address the confusion, Peter stood up in front of the crowd and addressed them saying:

[14] … "Men of Judea and all who dwell in Jerusalem, let this be known to you, and give ear to my words. [15] For these people are not drunk, as you suppose, since it is

only the third hour of the day. [16] But this is what was uttered through the prophet Joel:

[17] "'And in the last days it shall be, God declares, that I will pour out my Spirit on all flesh, and your sons and your daughters shall prophesy, and your young men shall see visions, and your old men shall dream dreams; [18] even on my male servants and female servants in those days I will pour out my Spirit, and they shall prophesy. (Acts 2)

Speaking on behalf of the believers, and in their defence, Peter told the crowd that what was taking place that day was a fulfilment of prophecy. Joel foretold of a day when the Spirit of God would be poured out on all flesh. The term "all flesh" is important. Peter identifies sons, daughters, young and old men, male servants and female servants as an example of what he is speaking about (see verses 17-18). There would be no more social distinctions. The Lord God would fill people of all social standings. He would fill the priests, prophets and kings but also their sons, daughters and even their servants. God was breaking down social barriers.

We can also understand from what Peter was saying that the term "flesh" referred not just to social standing but also to racial background as well. The fact that God chose to impart gifts of foreign tongues to these believers showed that he was willing to pour out His Spirit on Gentiles who came to Him as well. The message of the gospel was for all social and racial groups.

Peter's use of Joel is also significant in what it tells us about the words the believers spoke that day in those foreign tongues. He told the crowd that Joel foretold of a time when the Spirit of God would fill all flesh, and they would prophesy. This, according to Peter, is what was happening. Believers were prophesying in foreign tongues, declaring the wonders of God. Nations gathered in Jerusalem, were hearing in their own language the might works of the God of Israel.

What do we learn about the gift of tongues in Acts 2? Let me summarize what this passage shows us.

First, the tongues the believers who gathered at Pentecost spoke were known languages of the day. This is confirmed by those who heard them speak and listed the languages in which they spoke. They were distinguishable one from another, and those who spoke those languages heard about the mighty works of God in their native tongue.

Second, the tongues in which these early believers spoke were miraculously given, just as they were at Shinar at the Tower of Babel. The believers who spoke had not previously spoken these languages. The Spirit of God, who fell on them, gave them this ability. Speaking these tongues had nothing to do with their ability to learn languages but rather with the presence of the Spirit upon them.

The believers who spoke in tongues that day spoke prophetically. They did this by publicly declaring the wonders of God as the Spirit inspired them. They also did this by revealing the purpose of God to proclaim the gospel to the Gentile world in their language. By speaking out the gospel in these various languages, they were showing God's intention for not only the Jew but also for the Gentile. It was a declaration that the Spirt of God had come to bring the message of salvation to the whole world.

CHAPTER 3 -
The Commission of Jesus

In the last chapter, we saw how the believers who gathered together at Pentecost began to speak in other languages miraculously. Peter defended what was happening that day by referring to the prophecy of Joel concerning the coming of the Holy Spirit (see Acts 2:17-21, Joel 2:28-32). The prophecy of Joel, though important when it comes the matter of God pouring out His Spirit on the believers of the day, does not speak directly to this matter of speaking in various tongues. Joel talks about prophesying, visions and dreams but not about the what was of concern for the crowd that day –the speaking in tongues.

From what Peter said that day, we can assume that he understood that this miraculous gift of communicating in a language unknown to the speaker, was evidence of the pouring out of the Spirit. The question, however, remains: Does Scripture prophecy about this gift of tongues before the events of Acts 2? Is there more specific evidence in Scripture that points to this gift as being part of what God's Spirit would do when he fell on His people.

To answer this, we need to go to the Gospel of Mark. Listen to Mark's account of the Great Commission of Jesus as recorded in Mark 16:

> [15] And he said to them, "Go into all the world and proclaim the gospel to the whole creation. [16] Whoever believes and is baptized will be saved, but whoever does

not believe will be condemned. [17] And these signs will accompany those who believe: in my name they will cast out demons; they will speak in new tongues; [18] they will pick up serpents with their hands; and if they drink any deadly poison, it will not hurt them; they will lay their hands on the sick, and they will recover." (Mark 16)

The New International Version of the Bible adds a note prior to this section of the book of Mark:

"The most reliable early manuscripts and other ancient witnesses do not have Mark 16:9-2."

(The Holy Bible, New International Version: "Note on Mark 16:9-20", Grand Rapids: Zondervan Publishing House, 1984)

Even though not all ancient manuscripts contain this section, the NIV includes it in the text. The King James Version, New King James Version, English Standard Version and New Living Translation all include this passage of Scripture without any translation note, stating that they believe it to be part of the inspired Word of God. The text that concerns us here is Mark 16:15-18. Everything spoken of in these verses is either recorded in the other gospels or backed up by other Scripture, so we have no cause to doubt what it teaches. It is as authoritative as any other passage of Scripture and speaks the truth to us.

Let's consider now what the Lord said to His disciples in this passage. Here Jesus commissioned His disciples to go into all the world to preach the gospel and baptize those who believed what they taught. The Lord Jesus would not leave them alone to accomplish this task. He would pour out His Spirit on them and protect them as they went.

Listen to what the Lord Jesus told His disciples in Mark 16:17-18:

[17] And these signs will accompany those who believe: in my name they will cast out demons; they will speak in new tongues; [18] they will pick up serpents with their hands; and if they drink any deadly poison, it will not hurt them; they will lay their hands on the sick, and they will recover." (Mark 16)

There would be clear evidence of the presence and protection of the Lord on the disciples as they went out to the world to preach the gospel. The disciples would be given the power to cast out demons and heal the sick (see Acts 5:16). They would pick up serpents with their hands and not be harmed. We have a clear example of this in Acts 28:3-5 when Paul was in Malta, and a venomous snake bit him. He simply shook it off and suffered no ill effects. Jesus went on to say in Mark 16:18 that believers would drink deadly poison, and it would not hurt them. In Luke 10, Jesus sent out seventy-two disciples to preach the gospel. When they came back to him, they marvelled at the power that had been given to them to overcome the enemy. Listen to the words of Jesus to these returned evangelists:

Behold, I have given you authority to tread on serpents and scorpions, and over all the power of the enemy, and nothing shall hurt you. (Luke 10:19)

Jesus repeats in Mark 16 what he had already told them in Luke 10.

There is one more sign that I have purposefully left out until now. Notice in Mark 16:17 that Jesus told his disciples that they would also "speak in new tongues." Let's examine this phrase in the context of what Jesus was saying.

23

There are those who would say that the new tongues referred to here are the languages that the disciples of Jesus would learn to preach the gospel to foreign nations—not unlike what any missionary of our day must do in a language school. As a missionary, myself, I had to go through that process of learning a new language, but is this what the context of the verse is speaking about?

To understand what Jesus is saying here, we need to see two things in the context of these verses. Notice first that Jesus speaks here about "signs." The Greek word used here is "semeion," which refers to a mark, token or miracle. It is a proof of validity or a seal of authority. When Jesus said that speaking in new tongues was a sign, He was telling His people that there was a spiritual aspect to this ability. It was a miraculous occurrence that proved that they spoke in the name of the Lord. It appears to be much more than spending two years of hard human effort to learn a language. This was a spiritual gift given in a miraculous way to the servant of God. This is confirmed in Acts 2 when the disciples simply began to speak in foreign languages without prior study of these languages.

Notice secondly how speaking new tongues is in the context of other miraculous signs. Jesus told His disciples that they would speak new languages, pick up serpents in their hands, drink deadly poison, and it would not harm them, and lay hands on the sick and they would be healed. These signs were miraculous and pointed to the fact that those who demonstrated them were being protected and empowered by God.

Jesus confirmed the gift of tongues in Mark 16. He made it clear that the day was coming when those who believed in His name would speak new tongues as a sign from God that they were empowered for the work of the gospel.

It is important to mention, that in Mark 16:15-18, Jesus is speaking in a very general way about those who believed in His name. He is not saying that everyone who believes in His name will pick up serpents. Nor is He saying that everyone who believes in His name will drink poison and not be harmed. Similarly, He is not saying that every believer will speak new tongues or cast out demons.

What Jesus is saying, however, is that in the days that were to follow, various signs would be evident among those who believed in His name. They would hear stories of those who picked up poisonous snakes and brushed them off unharmed. They would witness those who spoke in new tongues. They would experience healing from physical illness or release from demon affliction as believers laid hands on the oppressed. While not everyone who believed would experience all these signs, the church would be empowered by this means to preach the gospel and expand the kingdom of God on the earth.

CHAPTER 4 -
The Gift is Given to the Gentiles

To this point, we have seen how the gift of speaking other tongues was given to the Jewish Christians in Jerusalem at Pentecost. It is not until Acts 10 that we read about the gift again. This time, however, the gift is not given to Jewish Christians in Jerusalem but Gentile Christians in the region of Caesarea.

The context of Acts 10 is significant. We encounter a Roman military commander by the name of Cornelius. Cornelius was a generous man who gave to the poor in his community. He was also a religious man who prayed regularly to God. One day Cornelius had a vision from God. In this vision, an angel appeared to him and told him that God had seen his generosity and heard his prayers. The angel told Cornelius that he was to send men to the home of Simon the tanner in Joppa. There was a man in that home by the name of Peter. He was to invite Peter to his house.

While the angel was preparing Cornelius, God was also preparing Peter for this meeting. Peter had grown up in a tradition of Judaism. This tradition believed that salvation was for the Jew as the chosen people of God. If God was going to send Peter to the home of a Gentile, He would need to teach him that salvation was also for the Gentile.

Peter was on the roof of Simon the tanner's house. He had gone up there to pray. While on the rooftop, Peter had a vision. In this vision, he saw a sheet descending from heaven. In the sheet were all kinds of unclean animals and reptiles. A voice called out to him in his vision: "Rise, Peter; kill and eat" (Acts 10:13). Peter, a Jew who followed the law of Moses, refused to do so saying: "By no means, Lord; for I have never eaten anything common or unclean" (Acts 10:14). In response to this answer from Peter, the voice in his vision said: "What God has made clean, do not call common" (Acts 10:15). This happened three times.

Peter was perplexed about what he had seen and wondered what the vison meant. As he considered what God might be saying to him through this vision, three men came to the home, asking for Peter. The Lord spoke to him at that moment and said: "Rise and go down and accompany them without hesitation, for I have sent them" (Acts 10:20). Peter obeyed, and the men led him to the home of Cornelius.

Cornelius explained his vision to Peter and asked him to share the message God had given him. The apostle understood that God was asking him to tell these Gentiles about the Lord Jesus and the forgiveness of sin that was available to them through His death on the cross. The message touched Cornelius and those who were with him. The Spirit of God moved and fell on the Gentiles present that day (Acts 10:45). Notice what happened that day:

[45] And the believers from among the circumcised who had come with Peter were amazed, because the gift of the Holy Spirit was poured out even on the Gentiles. [46] For they were hearing them speaking in tongues and extolling God. Then Peter declared, [47] "Can anyone withhold water for baptizing these people, who have received the Holy Spirit just as we have?" [48] And he commanded them to be baptized in the name of Jesus

Christ. Then they asked him to remain for some days.
(Acts 10)

The Jewish Christians present were amazed that the Holy Spirit had fallen on the Gentiles. Notice that verse 46 begins with the word "for." This little word connects us with the proceeding statement. The believers were amazed that God had given His Holy Spirit to the Gentiles. How did they know that the Holy Spirit was given to Gentiles? The answer is in verse 46:

[46] For they were hearing them speak in tongues and
extolling God... (Acts10)

Evidence of the presence of the Holy Spirit among the Gentiles was in the gift of tongues given them that day. When the believers saw that the same Holy Spirit rested on the Gentile believers as on the Jewish believers, they understood that God accepted the Gentiles as His children as well. The result was that they baptized them in the name of the Lord Jesus and received them as brothers and sisters.

Another such occurrence took place in the city of Ephesus under the ministry of the apostle Paul. There Paul found a group of twelve men. From the context, we understand that these men were disciples or followers of John the Baptist. Verse three tells us that they were baptized "into John's baptism." What we need to understand here is that being a disciple of John did not make these twelve men Christians. Cornelius was a generous man who prayed, but he had not yet come to know the Lord Jesus. As followers of John, these disciples had heard about the Lord Jesus and looked to Him as the Messiah, but they may not have yet come to know the Lord Jesus personally nor understood the message of salvation.

When Paul met these disciples, he saw that they had an understanding about the Messiah, but something was missing. He asked them if they had received the Holy Spirit when they believed (Acts 19:2). The disciples told Paul that they had never heard that there was a Holy Spirit (Acts 19:2). This tells us something important about the disciples. Listen to what Paul said in Romans 8:9:

[9] You, however, are not in the flesh but in the Spirit, if in fact the Spirit of God dwells in you. Anyone who does not have the Spirit of Christ does not belong to him. (Romans 8)

Paul made it very clear that the evidence of salvation in the life of a believer is the presence of the Holy Spirit. Anyone who does not have the Holy Spirit does not belong to Christ. It is the Spirit of Christ in us that is our new life.

We meet here, a group of twelve men who believed that Jesus was the Messiah, but their belief about Jesus did not save them. They had the right idea, but there was no life in them. This gave the apostle Paul the opportunity to explain more fully to them the purpose of God for salvation in the Lord Jesus. We do not have the full discussion between Paul and these disciples of John, but the result was that they understood the work of Christ more fully. That day they became true believers and were baptized in the name of the Lord Jesus. The Spirit of God fell on them, and they began to speak in tongues and prophesied (Acts 19:6).

In the book of Acts, we see have three passages that mention the gift of tongues. The first reference in Acts 2 speaks to the time when the Spirit of God fell on the Jewish Christians in Jerusalem. In Acts 10, the Spirit fell on Gentile believers in Caesarea. Acts 19 speaks about a group of twelve Jewish disciples of John who saw Jesus as the Messiah but had of yet to experience the reality of salvation. On each of these occasions, the Spirit of God revealed His presence through the gift of tongues.

While the gift of tongues was given on these three occasions, there is no other mention of the gift in the book of Acts. There are many records of people coming to faith in the Lord Jesus and receiving the gift of the Holy Spirit. Most of these references, however, make no mention of these believers speaking in tongues.

The other detail that is significant in the book of Acts is that on each occasion when the gift of tongues was given, it was to a different group (Jews, Gentiles and disciples of John). The gifts of tongues seemed to be a sign to the church that the Spirit of God had accepted members of these groups as His children. God was revealing His purpose to the church through the gift of tongues. He was showing them that He was restoring to Himself what He had separated at the Tower of Babel.

Notice the words of those who spoke in tongues in the book of Acts. In Acts 2, the Jews declared the mighty works of God (Acts 2:11). In Acts 10, the Gentiles extolled or praised God. In Acts 19, the disciples of John the Baptist spoke in tongues and prophesied. These early believers declared God's praise and spoke His heart through the gift of tongues, as given by the Holy Spirit.

In Acts 2, we have a reference to the various languages the believers spoke. On that occasion, we also have foreigners in the city of Jerusalem who heard the message of the gospel in their own tongue. In Acts 10 and 19, however, we have no indication that the gift of tongues was used in this way. In Acts 10, the gift of tongues was spoken in the context of a private meeting between the apostle Peter and the friends and family of Cornelius. Paul was with twelve disciples of John the Baptist in Acts 19. There is no reference to any foreigner present in Acts 10 or 19 to hear the gospel or the praise of God in their language.

As the apostle Paul and his co-workers went from town to town, we have no mention of the use of the gift of tongues as a miraculous gift being used to communicate the gospel in the different languages of the people they met. While we cannot necessarily rule this out, apart from Acts 2, there is simply no evidence of the gift of tongues being used regularly by the early church to evangelize foreigners in their own language.

There are those who believe that the gift of speaking tongues is the ability to learn a foreign language to reach the nations for the Lord. The problem with this is that there is no Biblical evidence for this. The book of Acts does not teach that the gift of tongues was an ability to learn a language but the supernatural ability to speak a language that was unknown to the speaker instantaneously. It was not a learned language, but one given by the Spirit in a moment.

What is clear from the book of Acts is that the gift of tongues was a gift given to various people in society to prove that God had accepted them as His children. The apostles, seeing this gift, identified it as a sign that God had accepted not just those who physically spoke in tongues as His children, but also the cultural group to which they belonged (Jews or Gentiles) as being a people God accepted.

CHAPTER 5 - General Guidelines About Spiritual Gifts

We come now to the teaching of the apostle Paul about spiritual gifts in 1 Corinthians 12. While what Paul has to say here is not exclusively about the gift of tongues, the principles he teaches are essential if we are to understand the use of the gift in general. Let's take a moment to consider the instructions Paul gives the Corinthians about their spiritual gifts and see what this teaches us about the use of the gift of tongues.

"I do not what you to be uninformed" (1 Corinthians 12:1)

Notice as the apostle begins his teaching on spiritual gifts, he makes the following statement:

[1] Now concerning spiritual gifts, brothers I do not want you to be uninformed" (1 Corinthians 12)

This verse sets the tone for what Paul is going to say. For the apostle, it was important that every Christian know and understand God's purpose for spiritual gifts. God gave these gifts for the good of the body of Christ and the expansion of His kingdom on the earth. They are the tools of our trade, and every Christian is to know about these tools if they are to be effective in the service of the Lord.

There are varieties of gifts, services and activities (1 Corinthians 12:4)

The apostle goes on in verse 4 to tell the Corinthians that there is a variety of gifts:

[4] Now there are varieties of gifts, but the same Spirit; [5] and there are varieties of service, but the same Lord; [6] and there are varieties of activities, but it is the same God who empowers them all in everyone. (1 Corinthians 12)

Paul speaks here in these verses about gifts, services and activities. The Greek word used for gift is the word "charisma," which, in this case, refers to spiritual gifts. The word service comes from the Greek word "diakonia" from which we get the word deacon. The idea here may be that there are various roles given to believers for the work of the kingdom (i.e. elders, deacons, evangelists, etc.). Finally, the word "activities" comes from the Greek word "energema" from which we get the word energy. "Energema" refers to the power of God's work and the result it produces.

What is crucial for us to understand here is that God is not limited to working in any one way. He has given a variety of spiritual gifts. He has established and anointed people to fulfil various offices in the church. He also demonstrates His power in miraculous and unexpected ways with or without the use of our gifts and offices.

No two gifts will be the same. You may have a gift of teaching, but that gift will differ from the same gift in a brother or sister. How we exercise our gift, what or who we teach, or even how we teach will vary from person to person. For this reason, it is vital that we seek the Lord in how and where we are to use our spiritual gifts. While it is helpful to learn from others who have the same spiritual gift, it is also vital that we learn what God intends for us.

While our gifts may vary, and no two gifts will look the same, Paul tells the Corinthians that it is the same Spirit who empowers all these gifts. This is an important principle for us to understand. It would be easy to judge another person because his or her gift is not the same as ours. Remember, however, that while no spiritual gift is the same, God is still the giver. We must expect diversity, but we must also understand that God is behind this diversity in the body.

To each is given the manifestation of the Spirit (1 Corinthians 12:7)

In 1 Corinthians 12:7, Paul tells the Corinthians that each person is given a manifestation of the Spirit.

[7] To each is given the manifestation of the Spirit for the common good. [8] For to one is given through the Spirit the utterance of wisdom, and to another the utterance of knowledge according to the same Spirit, [9] to another faith by the same Spirit, to another gifts of healing by the one Spirit, [10] to another the working of miracles, to another prophecy, to another the ability to distinguish between spirits, to another various kinds of tongues, to another the interpretation of tongues. [11] All these are empowered by one and the same Spirit, who apportions to each one individually as he wills. (1 Corinthians 12)

Notice in these verses the variety of gifts God gives.

1) The utterance of wisdom
2) The utterance of knowledge
3) Faith

4) Healing
5) Miracles
6) Prophecy
7) Distinguishing between Spirits
8) Various kinds of tongues
9) Interpretation of tongues

The list Paul gives here is not an exhaustive list of spiritual gifts and services. It is merely an example of what he has been teaching about the multiple ways in which God equips and uses His servants. Notice the reference to "various kinds of tongues." It is vital that we note this because it shows that the gift was still being given by God to the church at the time Paul wrote to the Corinthians. Paul lists it here as one of the ways in which God was equipping the church to minister to the "common good" (verse 7) of the body.

Another important detail we need to see in verses seven to eleven it that Paul begins by saying: "To each is given the manifestation of the Spirit" (verse 7). From this phrase, we understand that each believer is given a manifestation of the Spirit. If you are a believer today, the Spirit of God lives in you. He has empowered you in a particular way for the work of the kingdom. No one is excluded from this. When the Spirit of God comes to dwell in you, He comes to empower and enable you to serve the Lord Jesus. He imparts to every believer a unique "manifestation." A manifestation is a clear evidence of the presence and power of God in us. This manifestation is for the common good of the body of Christ. Paul's partial list of spiritual gifts is an example of some of the manifestations of the Spirit in the life of a believer. The challenge for us is to discover that manifestation and learn to make use of it.

There is one more detail I would like to mention from verses 7-10. Notice in verse 10 that the apostle adds the interpretation of tongues to the list of spiritual gifts. This is the first time this gift is mentioned in Scripture. Paul says nothing about it in 1 Corinthians 12, but it appears to be the ability to interpret the various tongues spoken, so the body of Christ is edified. We will touch on this further in another chapter.

A Variety of Gifts is Necessary for the Functioning of the Body (1 Corinthians 12:14-19)

In 1 Corinthians 12:14-19, Paul told the Corinthians that a variety of gifts and services were necessary for the body to function as God intended. To illustrate this, he used the example of the human body.

[15] If the foot should say, "Because I am not a hand, I do not belong to the body," that would not make it any less a part of the body. [16] And if the ear should say, "Because I am not an eye, I do not belong to the body," that would not make it any less a part of the body. [17] If the whole body were an eye, where would be the sense of hearing? If the whole body were an ear, where would be the sense of smell? [18] But as it is, God arranged the members in the body, each one of them, as he chose. [19] If all were a single member, where would the body be? [20] As it is, there are many parts, yet one body. (1 Corinthians 12)

Consider what the apostle is saying here. Imagine that the foot looked at that hand and saw how useful it was. Imagine that the foot said, "I don't have the flexibility of the hand. I can't pick up things. I can't write. I can't paint or hold a hammer. What use am I? Imagine the ear looking over to the eye and saying: "I can't see the light or colour.

I can't see the beauty of creation around me. I am inferior to the eye. I don't belong on this body."

Paul went on to say: "if an ear, where an eye, where would be the sense of hearing" (verse 17). You see, the ear does not function as an eye for a reason. It is designed to hear sounds. Those sounds are important and enable communication and warn us of danger. The ear does not look like the eye, nor does it function like the eye. If it could think it would not think like the eye. It does one thing, and the eye does another. What is important, according to Paul, is that the eye and the ear work together for the good of the whole body. They don't look the same, act the same, or think the same, but they are partners serving the common good of the body.

We often see things through the eyeglasses of our spiritual gifts. I remember being in a church where that pastors were keen evangelists. This was their passion and gifting. Every message we heard had to do with winning the lost. Every challenge had to do with going out and witnessing to our neighbours. There were times when the congregation felt guilty because they were not doing what the pastors were doing. While it is crucial that we share the gospel, if all we did was share the gospel, what would happen to those who came to the Lord? You see, we need people to share the gospel, but we also need people to disciple and teach those who come to Christ. We need people to encourage them in their pain and suffering. We need people to reveal Christ in worship. We need those who will stand with them in their need through practical support. No church will be healthy if only one gift is used. Every gift is required if the body is to function as the Lord intended.

Every gift is valuable (1 Corinthians 12:21)

Knowing that there are a variety of gifts can often lead to comparison. Admittedly, some parts of our body are not as necessary as others. You can lose a finger and still be in good health. To lose a leg or the use of your eyes would be more problematic. If the lungs, brain or heart were to stop working, we would die. Parts of our body provide more essential services. This is also the case for the church. For the body to function at full capacity, every part needs to be healthy. If we chose to get rid of every part of our body that was non-essential to life, what would life be like? Without the ability to see, hear, smell, walk, or touch, would we reach our potential?

What Paul is saying here is that if we discourage the use of spiritual gifts we don't understand or appreciate, we will never be all that God intends us to be. Listen to how the apostle explains this to the Corinthians:

[21] The eye cannot say to the hand, "I have no need of you," nor again the head to the feet, "I have no need of you." [22] On the contrary, the parts of the body that seem to be weaker are indispensable, [23] and on those parts of the body that we think less honourable we bestow the greater honour, and our unpresentable parts are treated with greater modesty, [24] which our more presentable parts do not require. But God has so composed the body, giving greater honour to the part that lacked it, [25] that there may be no division in the body, but that the members may have the same care for one another. [26] If one member suffers, all suffer together; if one member is honoured, all rejoice together. (1 Corinthians 12)

All gifts God gives to the church are valuable and serve a unique role in the expansion of His kingdom.

No one has all the gifts (1 Corinthians 12:27)

There is a final point I want to emphasize in 1 Corinthians 12. Listen to Paul's words in 1 Corinthians 12:27-28:

[27] Now you are the body of Christ and individually members of it. [28] And God has appointed in the church first apostles, second prophets, third teachers, then miracles, then gifts of healing, helping, administrating, and various kinds of tongues. (1 Corinthians 12)

Paul continues to remind the Corinthians of the variety of gifts and services in the body. He lists eight gifts and services in these verses:

1) Apostles
2) Prophets
3) Teachers
4) Miracles
5) Healing
6) Helping
7) Administrating
8) Various kinds of tongues

Having listed these eight gifts and services, the apostle went on to say:

[29] Are all apostles? Are all prophets? Are all teachers? Do all work miracles? [30] Do all possess gifts of healing? Do all speak with tongues? Do all interpret? [31] But earnestly desire the higher gifts. (1 Corinthians 12)

Paul asked the Corinthians two set of questions here? The first related to service positions in the church: "Are all apostles? Are all prophets? Are all teachers?" The answer to these questions was so obvious to Paul that he doesn't feel the need to answer. No, not everyone is an apostle.

Not everyone is a prophet. God gives these roles to certain people for the good of the church.

Paul then asks a similar set of question about spiritual gifts. "Do all work miracles? Do all possess the gifts of healing? Do all speak with tongues? Do all interpret?" The answer to this question is the same as the first set of questions. No, God does not give everyone the ability to perform miracles. Not everyone has gifts of healing. Not everyone speaks with tongues. Not everyone can interpret tongues. God disperses these spiritual gifts as He sees fit. Each person has a different gift and ministry.

What does 1 Corinthians 12 teach us about the gift of tongues? First, God wants us to be informed about this gift in the church (1 Corinthians 12:1). That is why I am preparing this study. Speaking in tongues is listed among the spiritual gifts God gives to the church, and so we need to understand more fully what this gift is and how the Lord wants to use it.

Second, just because we do not understand the gift and can survive without it does not mean that we can banish it from our churches. Paul tells us that all gifts are given for the common good, and if God gives this gift, it serves a purpose. It is essential that we accept what God gives and learn to use it for His glory and the expansion of the Kingdom.

Third, the fact that Paul puts the gift of tongues in his list of gifts is important. It tells us that years after Pentecost, the Lord was still empowering people with this ability. Paul recognized it as a legitimate gift and one that served an essential function in the body of Christ.

Paul not only lists the gift of tongues in his list of gifts but expands it by adding the gift of interpretation of tongues.

41

The gift of tongues and the interpretation of those tongues would work together to be an encouragement and blessing to the body of Christ. We will examine this in more detail in this study.

Finally, Paul makes it clear in 1 Corinthians 12 that the gift of tongues is not given to everyone. This is important because some believers insist that the only manifestation that shows whether a person has the Spirit of God is this gift of speaking in tongues. Paul makes it clear that each person is given a demonstration of the Spirit, but that demonstration varies from person to person. Not every Spirit-filled Christian will be able to speak in tongues, but all will be empowered to serve the King.

CHAPTER 6 -
They Will Cease

In 1 Corinthians 12, the apostle Paul wrote to the church in Corinth to teach them about spiritual gifts. 1 Corinthians 13 needs to be seen in this context. 1 Corinthians 13 is the famous chapter on love. We often take it out of context, however. Paul continues in this chapter to teach the Corinthians about spiritual gifts and the use of spiritual gifts in the church. He reminds them that if they are going to use their spiritual gifts, they are to do so in love.

In the book of 1 Corinthians, there is clear evidence that the church of Corinth was struggling with division. Paul begins his letter with the following statement:

[10] I appeal to you, brothers, by the name of our Lord Jesus Christ, that all of you agree, and that there be no divisions among you, but that you be united in the same mind and the same judgment. [11] For it has been reported to me by Chloe's people that there is quarrelling among you, my brothers. [12] What I mean is that each one of you says, "I follow Paul," or "I follow Apollos," or "I follow Cephas," or "I follow Christ." [13] Is Christ divided? Was Paul crucified for you? Or were you baptized in the name of Paul? (1 Corinthians 1)

This division in the church of Corinth was creating a serious problem. We see evidence of this division in 1 Corinthians 12 where Paul used the illustration of the human body to remind the Corinthians that every spiritual gift was important and that they were not to look down on those whose gift did not appear to be as important as theirs.

It is for this reason that Paul takes the time to speak about the importance of love in the use of spiritual gifts. Paul begins chapter 13 by talking to the Corinthians about the use of spiritual gifts without love:

[13:1] If I speak in the tongues of men and of angels, but have not love, I am a noisy gong or a clanging cymbal. [2] And if I have prophetic powers, and understand all mysteries and all knowledge, and if I have all faith, so as to remove mountains, but have not love, I am nothing. [3] If I give away all I have, and if I deliver up my body to be burned, but have not love, I gain nothing. (1 Corinthians 13)

Notice that Paul speaks about four spiritual gifts here:
1) Speaking in Tongues
2) Prophecy
3) Knowledge
4) Faith

To listen to someone speak in tongues without love, said Paul, is like listening to a noisy gong or a clanging symbol—it is irritating and serves no purpose. The same is said for prophecy, knowledge and faith. Love empowers these spiritual gifts. Love ought to be the motivation for the use of every manifestation of the Spirit.

Love is not always the motivation behind the exercising of spiritual gifts. I have met people who speak in tongues (whether from God or not) simply because they want to show others they can do so. The motivation behind this is not love for God or fellow believer but a selfish desire to be noticed. This is not the way to exercise spiritual gifts. The test of whether we are using our spiritual gifts correctly is this –are they used out of love for God and our brothers and sisters in Christ? To help people understand whether they are using their spiritual gifts in love, Paul defines love in 1 Corinthians 13:4-7:

[4] Love is patient and kind; love does not envy or boast; it is not arrogant [5] or rude. It does not insist on its own way; it is not irritable or resentful; [6] it does not rejoice at wrongdoing, but rejoices with the truth. [7] Love bears all things, believes all things, hopes all things, endures all things. (1 Corinthians 13)

From these verses, we can develop a series of questions to determine whether I am exercising my spiritual gifts in love. In the context of our study on the gift of tongues, Paul is offering us these questions to determine the motivation behind the use of our gift:

1) Am patient and kind in the use of my gift? (verse 4)
2) Am I speaking with a boastful or arrogant heart? (verse 4)
3) Am I being rude and insisting on people listening to me regardless of the context? (verse 5)
4) Do I have an irritable or resentful attitude when I speak? (verse 5)
5) Do I have a heart for truth and righteousness? (verse 6)
6) What happens when people do not listen to me? Do I bear with them, believe and hope in God, and endure their rejection with a godly attitude? (verse 7)

Asking ourselves these questions can help us to determine whether we are trusting God and acting in love when we use our spiritual gift. According to Paul, this applied to the use of all gifts and not just tongues, prophecy, knowledge and faith, as mentioned in 1 Corinthians 13:1.

In 1 Corinthians 13:8, Paul reminded the Corinthians that while spiritual gifts will one day come to an end, love will go on into eternity.

[8] Love never ends. As for prophecies, they will pass away; as for tongues, they will cease; as for knowledge, it will pass away. [9] For we know in part and we prophesy in part, [10] but when the perfect comes, the partial will pass away. [11] When I was a child, I spoke like a child, I thought like a child, I reasoned like a child. When I became a man, I gave up childish ways. [12] For now we see in a mirror dimly, but then face to face. Now I know in part; then I shall know fully, even as I have been fully known. (1 Corinthians 13)

Notice that the apostle tells us in these verses that prophecies, tongues and knowledge will cease and pass away. This has led some to conclude that the gift of tongues is no longer for today. Let's take a moment, however, to examine what Paul is saying in these verses.

We cannot separate the gift of tongues from the other gifts mentioned in these verses. Paul tells us that prophecy, tongues and knowledge will all pass away. He explains this more fully in the context.

Speaking about prophecy, Paul says:

[9] For we know in part and we prophesy in part, [10] but when the perfect comes, the partial will pass away. (1 Corinthians 13)

Right now, we can only prophecy in part. We don't have all the details about what is to come and the purpose and will of the Father. "When the perfect come," said Paul, "the partial will pass away." In other words, when the Lord Jesus returns, and sin is banished, we will understand what we cannot know now. We will see the heart of God. No prophet will need to tell for we will walk perfectly in His will and know Him. When we are with Christ, we will speak with Him directly. There will no longer be any need for prophets or prophecy.

Paul went on in verse 11 to say:

[11] When I was a child, I spoke like a child, I thought like a child, I reasoned like a child. When I became a man, I gave up childish ways. (1 Corinthians 13)

Notice how Paul compares prophecy and tongues to a child speaking. If you have ever listened to a young child speaking, it is often difficult to understand. Their understanding of reality is limited. The day is coming, however, when the child is fully mature. At that point, childish conversation with limited understanding comes to an end. The conversation of a mature adult comes from experience and reality.

When do we reach this maturity? While I walk on this earth, I am still a child growing in spiritual maturity. I will not be fully mature until I am in the presence of God and free from sin and its effects on my life. When I have reached this point, I can put aside my childish speech and speak as one who truly understands.

Our understanding of God and His ways is limited here on this earth. Like children, we try to grasp concepts that are too big for us to understand. God gives spiritual gifts to His servants to help us in our weakness. His prophets and teachers instruct us as He gives them understanding and revelation. He blesses others with the gift of tongues so they can pray and communicate His heart through interpreters.

Paul is telling us that as long as we are unable to express our hearts to God as we should, we will need the work of the Spirit. Until we can grasp the nature and purpose of God fully, we will need the gifts He imparts to the church.

In verse twelve, Paul went on to say:

[12] For now we see in a mirror dimly, but then face to face. Now I know in part; then I shall know fully, even as I have been fully known. (1 Corinthians 13)

Paul compares our knowledge to a person looking into a poor-quality mirror. The image reflected is blurry and unclear. This is what our knowledge of God and His purpose is like. We don't see Him clearly. We don't understand him fully. Our teachers explain the truth of God to us, but their understanding is also incomplete. They explain the best they can, but the details are never completely satisfying. There are still questions. The day is coming, said Paul when we will know even as we are known. We will know God, for we will see Him. We will be in His presence. There will no longer be a need for instructors to give us knowledge about God, for we will know much more than our greatest teacher on earth. We will no longer need prophets to tell us what He says for we will hear that directly from Him.

The day is coming when spiritual gifts will no longer be necessary. Those gifted with gifts of evangelism will no longer need to exercise their gift for all who live in the presence of Jesus will know Him. Those who have gifts of healing will no longer exercise their spiritual ministry for there will be no more sickness. The encouragers will no longer have reason to encourage. Counsellors will no longer need to counsel. The gifts God gives are for our use on this earth. As long as the perfect has not come, we will need these gifts. As long as we do not know God as He knows us, all these gifts will be necessary. When the perfect comes, and we are fully mature in Him, then the usefulness of these gifts will cease. Prophecy, tongues and knowledge, along with the other spiritual gifts God gives have an essential purpose on this earth, but their usefulness will cease when we are in the presence of God in heaven.

In 1 Corinthians 13, Paul continues to speak about the gift of tongues. It is not without reason that he uses this gift an example in this chapter about love. The gift of tongues has been a divisive gift for many believers. Paul challenged the Corinthians to be loving and compassionate toward each other and not allow this gift to divide us as children of God. In part, the purpose of this study is to reveal what the Bible says about the gift to help believers to be more understanding and loving toward each other.

A second point we need to make here is that love is to be the motivation behind speaking in tongues. While we cannot judge the motives and intentions of someone else, I believe that it is possible for us to desire this gift for other reasons than the love of God and fellow believers. It is irresponsible to desire to speak in tongues just so that people will think more highly of us. The only legitimate motivation that pleases God is love and devotion to Him. Those who have the gift of tongues must examine their practice and use of this gift to be sure they are using it out of love for God.

Thirdly, Paul seems to compare the gift of tongues to that of an immature child speaking to a father or mother. It appears from this that the reason we have this gift is because of our inability to pray or express ourselves to God as we ought. It is easy for those who speak in tongues to lift themselves above others because they have the gift. Paul is reminding us, however, that it is because of our weakness that God gives this ability.

Finally, 1 Corinthians 13 reminds us that the day will come when the gift of tongues will cease. When we have fully mature, and our ability to communicate with God is perfected, our childish speech will no longer be necessary. We will communicate with God with fluency and eloquence. We will express our heart and our devotion to Him without hindrance. What a day it will be when we can put aside this gift and communicate face to face!

It seems to me that we cannot use 1 Corinthians 13 to justify the idea that tongues in no longer a gift given to the church. Yes, it will one day cease, as will prophecy, instruction in knowledge, evangelism, healing and other gifts. Until the Lord returns, however, this and all other gifts of God's Spirit continue to be important and necessary.

CHAPTER 7 -
Paul's Teaching about Tongues

1 Corinthians 14 is the most significant passage in the Bible on the gift of tongues. In this chapter, Paul compares the gift of tongues to the gift of prophecy. In his comparison, the apostle reminds the Corinthians that the gift of tongues had its place, but prophecy was more useful for the body of Christ as a whole. This is primarily because tongues are not understood unless interpreted, while prophecy is spoken clearly so that everyone can benefit (see 1 Corinthians 14:1-3; 6, 10-11, 13, 23).

This teaching has led some to conclude that tongues are unnecessary. This is not the case. Paul is not in any way diminishing the significance of the gift of tongues in this passage. He is merely saying that each gift has its place. In public worship, the gift of tongues, without interpretation, has little benefit to the body.

It is clear from 1 Corinthians 12 that Paul recognized the significance of every spiritual gift:

[21] The eye cannot say to the hand, "I have no need of you," nor again the head to the feet, "I have no need of you." [22] On the contrary, the parts of the body that seem to be weaker are indispensable … (1 Corinthians 12)

No gift of God is insignificant. Every gift has its place and must be honoured. With this in mind, let's take a moment to consider what the apostle Paul teaches the Corinthians about the gift of tongues in 1 Corinthians 14.

Paul spoke in tongues

The first thing we need to see in 1 Corinthians 14 is that the apostle Paul had the spiritual gift of speaking in tongues. Listen to what he told the Corinthians in verse 18:

[18] I thank God that I speak in tongues more than all of you. [19] But in the church I would rather speak five intelligible words to instruct others than ten thousand words in a tongue. (1 Corinthians 14)

Notice this comparison between prophecy and tongues. Paul told the Corinthians that he preferred to speak a word of prophecy than to speak in tongues because prophecy would instruct them while tongues would only leave them confused. Having said this, however, the apostle makes it clear that he spoke in tongues more than all of them (verse 8). In other words, it was a regular occurrence for Paul. We have no record of Paul speaking in tongues in a public meeting, but it is evident that he did so quite often in private before the Lord.

Paul wanted the Corinthians to speak in tongues

Not only did Paul speak in tongues, but his experience of speaking in tongues was also such that he wanted all the Corinthians to experience this gift as well.

[5] I would like every one of you to speak in tongues, but I would rather have you prophesy. He who prophesies is greater than one who speaks in tongues, unless he

interprets, so that the church may be edified. (1 Corinthians 14)

While Paul seems to prefer the gift of prophecy, he told the Corinthians— "I would like every one of you to speak in tongues." Paul promotes the gift of tongues in this phrase. Although the gift had its place, it was nonetheless, something Paul wished every believer in Corinth could experience.

The one who speaks in tongues speaks to God

It is important that we understand why Paul tells the Corinthians that prophecy is more useful to the body than tongues. Listen to what he tells the Corinthians about the gift in verse 2:

[2] For anyone who speaks in a tongue does not speak to men but to God. Indeed, no one understands him; he utters mysteries with his spirit. (1 Corinthians 14)

"The one who speaks in tongues does not speak to men but to God," Paul told the Corinthians. This is an interesting statement when compared to the gift of tongues in Acts 2. In Acts 2, the foreigners who had come to Jerusalem heard the disciples speaking in a foreign tongue that they understood perfectly. Here in 1 Corinthians 1, Paul told the Corinthians, however, that the gift of tongues is not intended to communicate with other people but with God. The gift, as experienced by Paul and the Corinthians, appears to be a prayer language. This language was not used to communicate with other people. For this reason, its public use was of no particular benefit to the church. Unlike other spiritual gifts, this gift was best used in private.

53

Notice also for verse 2 that if a person spoke in tongues to another person, the person hearing would not understand what the tongue speaker was saying. It would be a foreign language to them. It would serve no purpose for someone to speak to another in tongues as they would not understand what was said.

The Spirit Prays but not the Mind

In 1 Corinthians 14:2, Paul told the Corinthians that the person who speaks in tongues, "utters mysteries with his spirit." Paul explained this more fully in verse 14 when he wrote:

[14] For if I pray in a tongue, my spirit prays, but my mind is unfruitful. (1 Corinthians 14)

Notice that Paul tells us that our spirit prays, but the mind of the tongue-speaker is unfruitful. In other words, the mind is disengaged. The words spoken were not the invention of the mind, nor does the mind understand the words. The words, however, are not unprofitable. They communicate with God, even though the mind is not aware of their meaning.

The concept of praying meaningful prayers without the mind being engaged is a difficult one for us to grasp. The reality of the matter, however, is that we often communicate or receive communication in ways that are not at all rational. Have you ever had a sense of danger lurking near-by even though you had no proof? Have you ever known something was going to change when there was no rational reason for that change? Have you ever sensed the leading of the Lord in a way that made no sense to you? Your rational mind told you that following that leading would be completely foolish. Have you ever done something simply because if felt right in your spirit and not because you were intellectually convinced that this was the proper step to take? Our spirit can communicate. Its communication is not necessarily rational and logical like our minds, but if we listen, we can hear the voice of our spirit. If our spirit can speak to us, surely it can also pour itself out to God as well, especially when God gives it a language to speak.

Tongues are not Understandable

In 1 Corinthians 14:6-1, Paul gives instructions about the public use of the gift of tongues.

[6] Now, brothers, if I come to you and speak in tongues, what good will I be to you, unless I bring you some revelation or knowledge or prophecy or word of instruction? [7] Even in the case of lifeless things that make sounds, such as the flute or harp, how will anyone know what tune is being played unless there is a distinction in the notes? [8] Again, if the trumpet does not sound a clear call, who will get ready for battle? [9] So it is with you. Unless you speak intelligible words with your tongue, how will anyone know what you are saying? You will just be speaking into the air. [10] Undoubtedly there are all sorts of languages in the world, yet none of them is without meaning. [11] If then I do not grasp the meaning of what someone is saying, I am a foreigner to the speaker, and he is a foreigner to me. (1 Corinthians 14)

In this passage, Paul uses four examples to show the Corinthians that speaking in tongues in public serves no purpose. Let's consider these examples.

First, Paul uses a personal example in verse 6. Imagine that he arrived at the church in Corinth and stood up to speak. As he spoke, he spoke in tongues for half an hour and then sat down. What benefit would the Corinthians receive from that half-hour? None of them would have understood what he said. Because they did not understand what he said, there would be no spiritual benefit to them at all.

Second, Paul uses an illustration of a musical instrument. Maybe you have had the experience of listening to someone learning to play an instrument (verse 7). The sounds they produce are unclear. Wrong notes are played as the "musician" fumbles with the keys or fingering. If each note is not clear and distinct from the other, then you have no way of knowing what tune is being played. The apostle compares speaking in tongues to the sound of someone trying to play a musical instrument without the necessary skill. The music doesn't make sense. It just sounds like a confusing noise. Using the gift of tongues in public, said Paul, is a confusing noise in the ears of those who listen. It is confusing and irritating.

The third illustration is that of a trumpet call to battle (verse 8). Imagine that a skilled trumpeter was called to sound the alarm for battle. As he takes the trumpet to his lips, he feels an inspiration to play a great tune of inspiration to the soldiers. He plays that tune with great skill and passion and puts down his trumpet. What is the response of the soldiers to his trumpet? They are soothed or inspired by his wonderfully played tune, but not one of them pick up his or her sword and prepare for battle. The reason for this is because the sound he played on the trumpet was not the call to action they understood. The result may be the loss of the battle. If what is communicated is not understood, then it is of no help to the listener and does not prepare them for the Master's call.

Finally, Paul speaks about the various human languages in the world. Each of the words uttered in those languages has a meaning. People who speak the language communicate effectively with each other. Suppose, however, you brought a believer from another country to share with you in your Sunday service. Imagine that he stood up and shared with you, in his language, an inspiring story of God's grace. You hear all the words and see the passion and joy on the face of this speaker, but because you do not understand his language, you have no idea of what he said. Any encouragement and blessing you could have received is forfeited because you do not speak his language. This, according to Paul, is what it is like for someone to speak in tongues in a public setting without an interpreter. No one understands what is said, and unless they understand there can be no blessing.

Tongues can be Interpreted

What we need to understand here is that not only do these who hear the tongues not understand what is said— neither does the one speaking in tongues! Paul told the Corinthians that the person speaking in tongues utters mysteries with his spirit (verse 2). Listen to what he says in verse 13:

> [13] For this reason anyone who speaks in a tongue should pray that he may interpret what he says. (1 Corinthians 14)

Notice what the apostle is saying here. He is telling the Corinthians that the person who speaks in a tongue, should pray that he may interpret what he says. In other words, the person speaking the words does not understand what he or she is saying unless they are given the ability by God to interpret those words. By telling the tongue-speaker to pray for the interpretation, Paul assumes that those who speak in tongues will not always have an interpretation of the words they are speaking.

The interpreting of tongues, however, opens the gift of tongues to a public setting. If the words can be interpreted, then they can benefit the larger body of Christ. In the next chapter, we will see what Paul has to say about the corporate use of tongues with an interpreter.

What does Paul teach us about the gift of tongues in this passage? Paul saw the gift of tongues as an important gift but one that had its proper place. Without an interpreter to explain the words, the gift of tongues had no benefit in a public meeting. No one can understand what was said, and no one would be encouraged or blessed by its practice.

Obviously, however, the private use of the gift had a great blessing for Paul. He told the Corinthians that he spoke in tongues frequently and wished that all believers could experience the gift. The apostle encouraged the private use of tongues and challenged believers to pray that God would give them an interpretation of what they were saying so that they could be further edified.

The question remains: Why does God enable people to speak in words they do not understand and require they pray for interpretation? Scripture does not answer this question for us. What is clear is that the gift has been given and this is the nature of the gift. If I were to speculate as to the reason, I suppose it might have to do with our minds and how they filter our thoughts and prayers. As much as I would like to think that I have the mind of Christ, I also recognize that my sinful thoughts get in the way. I find myself questioning what God is leading me to do. I find myself rationalizing and trying to find the logic behind everything.

Because I am such a logical and rational creature by nature, I filter everything the Lord is saying through that mindset. The problem with this is that the ways of the Lord are not my ways. He does not think the way I think. His purposes cannot be filtered through human logic. There are things about God and His ways that defy our reasoning.

By giving us a language we cannot understand, God bypasses all this reasoning and enables us to pray from our spirit, unhindered by my human logic. Because I do not understand the words I speak, I can pray without this hindrance from the core of my being as inspired by the Spirt of God who lives in me.

CHAPTER 8 -
The Public Use of Tongues

In the last chapter, we saw how Paul described the gift of tongues as a gift that seemed to bypass the mind. The individual who spoke in tongues was not aware of what he or she was saying and needed to pray that God would give them the interpretation. In the same way, those who heard someone speaking in tongues would not understand what the person was saying unless it was interpreted. Paul's conclusion seems to be that the use of tongues in the church without an interpretation was of no public benefit.

There are those who would conclude from this that the gift should not be used in public worship and is futile in private practice. This was not the opinion of the apostle Paul. Listen to what he told the Corinthians in 1 Corinthians 14:15:

> *[15] What am I to do? I will pray with my spirit, but I will pray with my mind also; I will sing praise with my spirit, but I will sing with my mind also. (1 Corinthians 14)*

If we do not understand what we speak, and the gift has no public benefit without an interpreter, what should we do with the gift? Paul answers the question by saying that he would pray with his spirit and pray with his mind. He would sing with his spirit but also with his mind as well. In other words, he would continue to use the gift of tongues in his personal life and pray with his spirit. He would not in the process, however, neglect his regular prayers where he thoughtfully brought his requests to God.

It is significant that the apostle not only speaks about praying with his spirit but also of singing with his spirit. This shows us that the use of tongues is not only in prayer but also in song. It is not without reason that in the Old Testament, there is a connection between prophecy and singing. Many of the prophecies of the Old Testament are written as poetry. It is quite possible that Paul not only prayed in tongues but also sang in tongues as well. While he may have sung in this God-given language, Paul would also sing praises to God with understanding and thoughtfulness. Paul's personal decision was to use his God-given gift in prayer and song without neglecting his regular times of prayer and worship. In other words, singing and praying in tongues was not a replacement for singing and praying with full understanding.

Regarding the public use of the gift, Paul told the Corinthians in 1 Corinthians 14:16, 17 that if they gave thanks to God with their spirit in a tongue, those who heard them would not be able to say "Amen" because they would not understand what they were saying. Paul did not doubt that the person was giving thanks to God, but that thanksgiving and praise did not build up the body because it was not understood.

[16] Otherwise, if you give thanks with your spirit, how can anyone in the position of an outsider say "Amen" to your thanksgiving when he does not know what you are saying? [17] For you may be giving thanks well enough, but the other person is not being built up. (1 Corinthians 14)

Paul was very thankful for his gift of tongue, but he told the Corinthians that he would rather speak five understandable words of prophecy in the church than ten thousand words in a tongue.

[18] I thank God that I speak in tongues more than all of you. [19] Nevertheless, in church I would rather speak five words with my mind in order to instruct others, than ten thousand words in a tongue.

It is clear from this that Paul delighted in and encouraged the use of tongues but recognized that this gift had its place. There was no purpose to the public speaking in tongues without an interpreter. If the whole church spoke publicly in tongues and an outsider came into their worship service, that outsider would be confused and say that they were out of their minds:

[23] If, therefore, the whole church comes together and all speak in tongues, and outsiders or unbelievers enter, will they not say that you are out of your minds? (1 Corinthians 14)

The outsider coming into such a church service would not be edified. He or she would not understand what was going on and would leave confused.

In 1 Corinthians 14:21-2, Paul quotes from Isaiah 28:11 to illustrate the response of unbelievers to Christians speaking in a foreign tongue:

[21] In the Law it is written, "By people of strange tongues and by the lips of foreigners will I speak to this people, and even then they will not listen to me, says the Lord." [22] Thus tongues are a sign not for believers but for unbelievers, while prophecy is a sign not for unbelievers but for believers. (1 Corinthians 14)

Here in these verses, the apostle reminded the Corinthians that Isaiah prophesied of a time of judgement for Israel. The day was coming when the Lord would send a foreign nation to destroy them. They would hear a language they did not understand walking down their streets. Those who spoke this language had come to take over their land and bring them into exile. When they heard that foreign language, they would know that the judgement of God had come. According to Isaiah, the sound of foreigners in their land did not make these Israelites turn to God. They continued in their evil path, confirming the wrath of God upon them.

What is Paul teaching about the use of tongues here? He is telling the Corinthians that the public use of tongues will have no positive effect on the unbeliever. Just as the Israelites did not change their ways when they heard foreigners in their land, neither would the gift of tongues spoken in front of unbelievers change their ways. If anything, this gift confirmed that they are under the judgement of God. What is the response of the unbeliever, hearing the praises of God in tongues? He or she walks away saying that those who spoke praise in a tongue were "out of their mind." This was a sign that they were not right with God and under His judgment.

While the public use of tongues without an interpreter was of no benefit either to the believer or the unbeliever, Paul does not rule out the blessing there could be for the church through the proper use of the gift. He concludes his teaching on this subject in verses 26-28 by offering some guidelines in the public use of the gift.

[26] What then, brothers? When you come together, each one has a hymn, a lesson, a revelation, a tongue, or an interpretation. Let all things be done for building up. [27] If any speak in a tongue, let there be only two or at most three, and each in turn, and let someone interpret. [28] But if there is no one to interpret, let each of them keep silent in church and speak to himself and to God. (1 Corinthians 14)

In these verses, Paul teaches the Corinthians about the various aspects of the worship service. He speaks about a hymn, a lesson, a revelation, a tongue and an interpretation. This shows us that the when the early church met together, they sang hymns of praise to God, they had a lesson from Scripture and they shared the things God was revealing to them (either through a prophecy or a tongue with interpretation). Focusing on the gift of tongues, Paul gives four principles for the public use of the gift in public.

First, the apostle told the Corinthians that everything was to be done for the edification of the body. Whether it was the singing, preaching or sharing, all activities performed in the church worship service were to build up the believers and encourage them in their spiritual walk with Christ. Any public use of the gift of tongues was to have this as its objective. If the gift is used to promote oneself or it is divisive in the church, then it is not being used for building up. This means that there are times when the gift could be legitimately used, but it is better to refrain from using it because it may cause division. This takes discernment and wisdom from God.

Second, Paul told the Corinthians that in any given worship service, the public speaking in tongues should be limited to two or at the most three people. It was important to give people time to sing praise and to listen to a message from God's Word. The gift of tongues had its place, but it was not to take over the worship and teaching service.

Third, Paul admonished those who spoke in tongues to speak each in turn. This meant that if someone was speaking publicly in a tongue, everyone else was to be quiet and allow that person to speak. They were not to all speak in tongues at the same time. Remember that Paul challenged the Corinthians to make it their ambition to see that everything be done for the building up of the body. He reminded them that speaking in tongues publicly without interpretation was not for the public good and edification. While tongues were not forbidden in worship, Paul told the Corinthians that they were to be spoken one person at a time in the worship service. According to Paul, it was not in the best interest of the church to have multiple people talking out loud at the same time.

Fourth, Paul required an interpretation of all tongues spoken publicly in the church. This interpretation might be given to the one who spoke, or it might be given to someone else who was given an understanding of the words spoken. What was important was that the church understood what God was saying. When the tongue was interpreted, it would bless or exhort the church. It was a means by which the Lord could speak to the whole body. This shows us yet another use of the gift of tongues. Very similar to prophecy, the gift of tongues can be a means by which God exhorts, encourages or builds up the church. For this to take place, however, an interpretation is required.

Paul goes on in verse 28 to say that if there is no one to interpret, the tongue-speaker was to keep silent in church. In other words, there was to be no public speaking in tongues in church unless there was an interpreter. Every tongue spoken publicly in the church was to be interpreted for the good of the whole body. If someone spoke in a tongue, and no one had an interpretation, that person was to sit down and remain quiet. He or she was to speak no further.

Notice what Paul told the tongue-speaker who had no interpretation in verse 28.

66

[28] But if there is no one to interpret, let each of them keep silent in church and speak to himself and to God. (1 Corinthians 14)

If there was no interpreter, the tongue-speaker was to keep silent and speak to himself and God. The phrase "keep silent and speak" is quite intriguing in this context. It shows us that Paul was not asking this individual to stop speaking in tongues but to stop speaking out loud and speak quietly to himself and God alone. This individual was to prayer in tongues quietly during the service but not speak out loud. Paul is not forbidding the private and quiet use of tongues in the worship service. He seems to be encouraging its private use in a way that was not disturbing others. Any public demonstration of the gift, however, required interpretation.

The apostle concludes his teaching on the use of tongues in public worship in verses 39-40 when he said:

[39] So, my brothers, earnestly desire to prophesy, and do not forbid speaking in tongues. [40] But all things should be done decently and in order. (1 Corinthians 14)

Notice two details in these verses. First, "do not forbid speaking in tongues." Paul is telling the Corinthians that speaking in tongues is a gift from God. They were not to forbid the practice of any gift that God gave His people. All gifts were necessary and served an essential purpose in the church.

The apostle went on to say secondly, "all things should be done decently and in order." It was the concern of Paul that the church seek harmony and the common good of the body. While the church was not to forbid the use of the gift of tongues, it was to insist on the proper use of the gift according to the principles he had laid out for them. No gift was to be forbidden, but the improper use of gifts would only create division and chaos.

Reading between the lines, we have a sense that the church in Corinth was struggling with balance in the use of this manifestation of the Spirit. The recommendations of Paul were not just for the church of Corinth but the church in general. The guidelines he presents here if followed, will move the church toward greater health and unity.

CHAPTER 9 -
An Attempt to Answer Questions

We have examined what the Scriptures teach about the gift of tongues. As we conclude this study, I would like to address a series of questions that will naturally be the result of what we have seen so far. Let me be clear before addressing these questions. There is a mystery to God and the gifts He gives. We will not have an answer to all our questions and will have to walk by faith in what Scripture teaches and how the Spirit of God leads. It seems to me that the practice of any gift will differ from person to person. How a person exercises the gift will be unique to each person.

The other matter I want to make clear is that we have no authoritative answers apart from Scripture. Where Scripture is silent on an issue, we can only speculate. Speculation is not authoritative; it is merely my opinion. My goal here in this study is only to deal with those questions that can be answered by Scripture.

Do I need to speak in tongues?

There are those who teach that speaking in tongues is a requirement for every believer and the evidence that a believer is filled with the Spirit. This, however, is not what the Scripture seems to teach. We have no record of Jesus ever speaking in tongues, though of all people He was undoubtedly filled with the Spirit.

In Mark 16:17 tells us that there will be signs accompanying those who believed. They would speak in now tongues, pick up serpents with their hands, cast out demons, and lay hands on the sick and they would recover. Some Christians use this passage to say that speaking in tongues is a sign that we truly believe. The problem with this is that we cannot take only one of these signs and apply it to all believers. Not everyone will drink poison and not be hurt. Not everyone will lay hands on the sick and see them healed. Not everyone will speak in new tongues. But there will be evidence of these signs in the life of the church as God gifts those He pleases with these various abilities.

In 1 Corinthians 12:29-31, the apostle Paul asks the question? "Do all speak with tongues" (verse 30). This question is in the context of a teaching about whether every believer is an apostle, prophet or teacher. The answer is so evident that Paul does not even answer the question. Of course, not everyone is a prophet or apostle. Not everyone has been called of God to be a teacher in the church. Nor, according to Paul, does everyone have the gift of tongues. God gives gifts to each as he chooses. We do not all have the same spiritual gifts and God-given abilities (see 1 Corinthians 12:15-20).

Speaking to the Corinthians in 1 Corinthians 14:5, the apostle Paul said: "I want you all to speak in tongues." The word "want" in the Greek language is "theleso" which means to will, to wish or to desire. It is not so much a command as a desire. Paul's experience with the gifts was such that he wanted every believer could experience it. Paul could hardly be commanding all believers to have this gift in this verse when in other verses he makes it clear that the gift is not for all believers but only to those to whom God gives it.

Clearly, believers at Pentecost spoke in tongues. It is also evident that Cornelius and those who were with him also spoke in tongues when they came to faith in the Lord Jesus. We also have a reference to the apostles of John the Baptist coming to faith and speaking in tongues. We read of three occasions in Scripture where those who believed spoke in tongues. For each of these verses, however, there are multiple passages in Scripture that speak of people coming to faith in Christ with no mention of speaking in tongues. We have clear evidence that some people spoke in tongues when they believe, but we cannot assume that this was the case for every believer who came to Jesus. We cannot apply the experience of one person to every believer. God works in different ways in each life.

In 1 Corinthians 12:4-11, the apostle Paul told the Corinthians that to each believer there was given a "manifestation of the Spirit" (verse 7). This manifestation was a sign that they belonged to God and were empowered by him. What is important for us to note here is that Paul makes it clear that not every believer had the same manifestation. Paul would go on to say that to one person the Spirit of wisdom, to another the Spirit of faith and to another the ability to speak "various kinds of tongues" (verse 10). He concludes this teaching but saying: "All these are empowered by the same Spirit, who apportions to each one individually as he wills" (verse 11).

The evidence or manifestation of the Spirit of God is not the same for everyone. There is no evidence in Scripture that every believer must speak in tongues. If anything, Scripture teaches that the gift of tongues, like every other gift, is given to those God chooses. Evidence of God's Spirit in us goes far deeper than the gift of tongues. The Spirit reveals His presence and power in multiple ways.

How do I receive the gift of speaking in tongues?

There are those who, upon reading this study, may wonder how they can receive the gift of tongues. The answer to this is the same for any gift. A gift by its nature is given freely to us through the generosity and gracious hand of the one who possesses it. The source of this gift and all others is God. He alone is the giver of all spiritual gifts. He gives as He pleases.

Knowing this should help us to understand that the gift of tongues is not something we try to obtain by our effort. Some believers are so desirous of having this gift that they attempt to imitate others or form non-sensical words by their own means. This is not the gift of tongues. The gift, as we see it in Scripture, was given to those who were not even expecting it. In an instant, they were speaking words that came from the Spirit. They were not doing this by their own means. They were surprised at what was taking place in them. It was not a learned behaviour; it was a gift given without personal effort or training.

Having said this, there is evidence in Scripture that indicates that we can pray for certain gifts from God. Paul told the Corinthians in 1 Corinthians 14:39 that they were to "earnestly desire" to prophesy. The fact that the Corinthians are encouraged to desire this gift implies that God was willing to impart the gift to those who wanted it. We also read in 1 Corinthians 14:13 that those who speak in tongues were to ask God for the ability to interpret what they spoke. Again, we see that God is willing to give words of prophecy or interpretations of tongues to those who seek Him.

How do I receive the gift of tongues? I do so by recognizing that all spiritual gifts come from God. Knowing this, I examine my motives in seeking such a gift. Paul tells us that all gifts are to be used for building up the body of Christ (see 1 Corinthians 14:26). The apostle James also tells us that we ask and don't receive because we ask wrongly, "to spend on it on your passions" (James 4:3). In other words, we can ask for things, not for God's glory but out of selfish motives. Those selfish motives do not build up the body of Christ but divide it. God is not obligated to give us any spiritual gift. Paul shows us that we can ask God for spiritual gifts but remember that with each gift comes greater responsibility for "everyone to whom much was given, of him much will be required" (Luke 12:48). The gift of tongues is not a toy or amusement to be played with but a tool for the service and expansion of the kingdom of God.

Is there evidence in Scripture that the gift has ceased?

The key passage we need to examine is 1 Corinthians 13:8, which says that tongues will cease as would knowledge and prophecy. In the context of 1 Corinthians 12-14, the apostle has been addressing the difference between prophecy and tongues and giving some guidelines regarding their place and use in the church. It is for this reason that these gifts are particularly mentioned. This, however, is not an exhaustive list of gifts that will cease.

Consider the office and gift of an evangelist. Of what use will the gift of evangelism be in heaven? We will all know the Lord. Consider the gift of mercy. How will it be possible to have mercy or compassion on someone whose life is complete and perfect with nothing lacking? In heaven, there will be no sickness or dying. What is necessary on this sin-cursed earth will not be necessary in heaven. Tongues, like evangelism, will no longer be needed when we are in the presence of the Lord Jesus.

1 Corinthians 13:9-12 makes it clear that "when the perfect comes," there will no longer be a need of these gifts. When I "shall know fully, even as I am known," I will no longer need a teacher to teach me, or a prophet to explain what I already know. As far as I can see, perfection has not come to this world, and I do not yet know Christ as I am known. I expect fully that the gift of tongues will cease but not until I see Christ and dwell in His presence. Then the gift will no longer be needed for I shall see Him, know Him and speak with him face to face. Until that time, God had given us spiritual gifts to use for the expansion of His kingdom and the building up of his church on this earth.

What it the purpose of tongues, and how does it build up the body of Christ?

If the gift of tongues is still given today, what is its purpose and how does it serve to build up the body of Christ. Let me summarize what we have examined in this study.

The gift that was given in Acts 2 was given as a sign to show the believers in Jerusalem that God was opening the door for the foreigner to come to Christ. That day, the Spirit of God moved believers and spoke through them in known languages, miraculously given, at a time when people from many nations were present in the city. God moved these disciples to preach and share the wonders of God with people of other nationalities, showing that His salvation was not just for the Jew. In this case, God gave the gift to expand the vision of the church.

As we move further into the book of Acts, we see how God caused Cornelius and the disciples of John to speak in tongues. Again, this was a clear sign to the church that God had put His spirit in these foreigners and accepted them as His own. The gift of tongue, in this case, confirmed to the church that what happened at Pentecost was being fulfilled in the lives of these foreigners. On this basis, the church was forced to accept these Gentiles as fellow believers.

In Paul's teaching in 1 Corinthians 14, we see how the gift of tongues was used by individuals to build themselves up -- "The one who speaks in a tongue builds up himself" (verse 4). Paul does not go into detail about how God uses the gift to build up the individual believer. This, I am sure would vary from person to person and depend on the circumstances in their life. God may grant interpretation to the tongue-speaker and by this means reveal His will or bring comfort and encouragement.

In 1 Corinthians 14:14, Paul speaks about praying in tongues God uses the gift to lead His servants to pray for His purposes around the world. Paul told the Corinthians that he would pray with his mind, but He also recognized the value of praying from His spirit in tongues. Just as He uses our ordinary prayers to accomplish His purposes in the church, so God uses our prayers in tongues to fulfil His plans.

Paul speaks of singing praise to God with his spirit in 1 Corinthians 14:15. The implication here is that the tongue-speaker can sin in tongues. This singing offers praise to God. Again, Paul told the Corinthians that he would also sing with his mind, but that singing with his spirit also brought praise to God.

1 Corinthians 14:16-17 speak of giving thanks in the spirit through tongues. Paul told the Corinthians that doing so in public was not blessing the body because they did not understand the words spoken. Listen, however, to what he said in verse 17: "… you may be giving thanks well enough, but the other person is not built up." Paul does not doubt that the tongue-speaker was giving thanks to God here. It is clear from this that another use of the gift of tongues is offering thanksgiving to God.

Finally, in 1 Corinthians 14:5, Paul told the Corinthians that the one who prophesied was greater than the one who spoke in tongues unless someone interpreted so that the body could be built up. This shows us that the gift of tongues, accompanied by an interpretation is one way in which God speaks prophetically to the body. Unlike prophecy, however, tongues require and interpretation to build up the church.

Why is the gift more evident in some Christian circles then others?

As we look around us at the Christian church, we see more evidence of the gift of tongues in some circles than others. Why is this the case if the gift is still being given today? Let me break my rule and speculate as to the reason for this.

First, the theology of some churches states that all who are filled with the Spirit must speak in tongues. While I do not believe this to be the teaching of Paul, this is nonetheless the teaching of these churches. If this is your belief, you will attract those who have been given the gift because they have a legitimate setting to use the gift.

Second, if you have been taught that you must speak in tongues or you are not Spirit-filled, you will earnestly desire the gift. This means that you will be praying to God and seeking this ability. We have seen that God is willing to give gifts to those who ask.

Third, as in any church, there will always be counterfeits. We have spoken about how it is possible to train yourself to speak non-sensical words and feel that you have the gift of tongues.

Fourth, there are other churches whose theology states that this gift has ceased. If you belong to this kind of church, you will not likely hear anyone speaking in tongues. If someone does, they may very quickly be silenced. You would not expect to see the gift of tongues in a church that believes that the gift is no longer given.

Finally, in other churches, the gift may be given, but it is not practiced in public worship. These churches prefer to refrain from using it publicly because it may be too divisive for the body. People with the gift use it privately or quietly to themselves in the worship service.

Why does God give a language we cannot understand? Can we trust a gift that bypasses the mind?

I suppose one of the most confusing things about the gift of tongues is that the Bible teaches that it is not understood unless there is an interpreter. The question that arises, therefore, is why God would give us the ability to speak with words we do not understand? The Bible does not give us an answer to this question. We can only speculate as to why God does what He does. Having said this, let me offer some personal suggestions.

First, as human being, we are quite logical. We filter everything through this logic. Naturally, we struggle to believe what we cannot explain. This, of course, is where faith in God is essential. I would venture to say that many of our prayers are filtered through our own ideas and preferences. We come to God telling Him what we want and persist in these prayers until we get our answer. There are times, however, when what we want is not what is best for us. Israel prayed for a king even through it was not in their best interest. Because they persisted in this request, however, God gave them a king. Sometimes the preferences and logic of our mind get in the way of what God wants to do. Being able to pray from our spirit without these obstacles may be why God gives us a language we cannot understand or manipulate for our purpose.

Second, in the Christian life, we need to understand that not all of God's ways are logical and reasonable to our earthly mind. God will ask us to do things that will not make sense to us. It did not make sense for David to face Goliath with a slingshot and a few stones (1 Samuel 17). I did not make sense for Gideon to reduce his army from 22,000 to three hundred to face the Midianites. Nor did it make sense to arm those men with empty jars, lights and trumpets, but that was the command of God (Judges 7). Did it make sense for Noah to build an ark on dry land with no body of water nearby? Did it make sense for Moses to lead over two million people into the desert without adequate provisions for the forty-year journey? Did it make sense for the disciples to follow the command of Jesus to feed a hungry multitude with a small boy's lunch? From a human perspective, these events did not make sense. God's ways are very different from our ways, and His logic is not like ours. If we only do what we understand and what makes sense to us, then we will miss out on the wonderful things He wants to do through us that defy human logic and reason.

A faith that only does what it logical and understandable to the human mind is not faith at all. Such a faith cannot expect the miraculous That is often where we are in our Christian life. We can explain everything. We can predict what will happen. We run our churches like businesses with attainable goals and strategies. We motivate people as any good advertiser would. We attract people by providing them with what they want. All this is attainable in the non-Christian world. All these techniques can be studied in a good book about worldly business. God is not looking for mindful and logical strategies that can be attained in human effort. He is looking for men and women who will step out beyond human reason and trust His leading to accomplish what cannot be explained apart from Him.

Can we trust a gift that bypasses the mind? If God is in it, we certainly can! The gift of tongues is not a reasonable and explainable language. You can't examine it and study its grammar. But then, how do you explain a miracle? How do you explain that one day you were lost in sin and the next day you were transformed into a new person?

Many years ago, I was speaking to a man who told me that he had a problem with the doctrine of the trinity. It did not make sense to him. "How can God be one and three people at the same time?" he asked. I remember the response the Lord gave me for him at that time. "Leo," I said, "I am glad that there are things about God I cannot understand. If I could understand everything about Him, then He would be no bigger than my brain. I need a God that I cannot understand. I need a God that is bigger than me."

We have a God who is bigger than our human logic. There are things about Him we cannot explain. His purposes defy our understanding. Those whose faith has become so logical that they cannot accept what they cannot explain will fall short of God's purpose.

How do I know if the gift is genuine? Are their counterfeits?

As with any gift, there will always be the potential of counterfeits. I have heard of individuals who, attempting to be accepted as a "Spirit-filled believer" in their church, have made efforts to learn how to speak words they called tongues. This language, however, was made up in their mind and not a language given by the Spirit.

Wherever the Lord is working, we can be sure that the presence of the enemy will also be there. It is possible that someone could speak words given to them by demonic forces to hinder the work God is doing. We cannot underestimate the power of the enemy to infiltrate our ranks with counterfeit gifts.

How can we have some assurance that the gift of tongues is genuine? Let me offer two suggestions here.

First, Paul challenges those who speak in tongues to pray for the ability to interpret. He also commands that anyone who speaks tongues in public be interpreted by and interpreter. This matter of interpretation is key in determining whether the gift of tongues is genuine or not. The apostle Paul had this to say about those who spoke in the Spirit:

[3] Therefore I want you to understand that no one speaking in the Spirit of God ever says "Jesus is accursed!" and no one can say "Jesus is Lord" except in the Holy Spirit." (1 Corinthians 12)

Paul makes it clear that no evil spirit of hell will every say, "Jesus is Lord." The thought is repulsive to them. Similarly, if what is spoken belittles or blasphemes the name of the Lord, we know that it is not from the Spirit. The test is very clear. If we pray for an interpretation, and the interpretation brings glory to God, we can have the assurance that it is from the Spirit. If on the other hand, the interpretation blasphemes Him or His purposes the tongues spoken are not from God.

A second test for the genuineness of the gift of tongues is an examination of the character of the person who speaks. Listen to what Jesus said in Matthew 7:

[17] So, every healthy tree bears good fruit, but the diseased tree bears bad fruit (Matthew 7)

If the person who speaks in tongues does not walk with the Lord, we need to be suspicious of what he or she is saying. God can still speak through these individuals, but we need to be careful. If you have no desire to walk with the Lord or honour Him, and you are speaking in tongues, you may need to ask the Lord if what you are saying is truly from Him.

Third, the apostle told the Corinthians that all things were to be done for the edification of the body of Christ. If the use of tongues is disrupting the worship of the church or causing division and chaos than it is either being used in the wrong way or does not come from God at all.

The final test, I would offer here is that test of motive. Speaking about the Pharisees of His day, the Lord Jesus said:

[5] They do all their deeds to be seen by others. For they make their phylacteries broad and their fringes long, [6] and they love the place of honour at feasts and the best

81

seats in the synagogues [7 and greeting sin the marketplaces and being called rabbi by others. (Matthew 23)

If you want to know if your use of the gift of tongues is genuine, examine your motive. Are you exercising this gift to be noticed, or are you being led by the Spirit? Is your desire for the glory of God and the building up of His church or your glory? While the gift may be genuine, its exercise may be wrong because of its wrong motive.

Let me say one more thing in this context. The gift of tongues is not the only gift that can be counterfeited. The early church dealt continually with false prophets and false teachers. Consider also that there are those who seem to have the gift of mercy and encouragement who are merely trying to gain a personal following. Every gift can be counterfeited. We cannot throw out all gifts simply because the potential exists for them to be used by Satan in our church. Instead, we must learn to discern truth from error. We must pull out the weeds so that those plant that produces good fruit are encouraged to full growth.

Can the person with the gift control it or is it something that just happens?

We have very little information in Scripture about the personal and private use of the gift of tongues. I suppose that this may have to do with the fact that the experience of the gift may vary from person to person. Not everyone with the same spiritual gift, whatever the gift might be, will use that gift in the same way. This is likely true for the gift of tongues as well.

The question I am addressing here is this: Can a person with the gift of tongues use or refrain from using the gift at will? Can a person with the gift, pray in tongues whenever they want, or must they wait for the Spirit of God to move them to do so?

The answer can be found in 1 Corinthians 14, where Paul speaks about orderly worship and the use of tongues. He speaks in this passage about two or three people at most speaking in a tongue with an interpreter. He told those who spoke in a tongue and found that there was no interpretation to sit down and be silent (see 1 Corinthians 14:28). This shows us that there as a control that was to be exercised by the individual in the use of their gift. They were responsible before God to refrain from speaking in tongues on certain occasions. They were also to be willing to speak in a tongue when the opportunity was right. It is clear from this that the Spirit of God does not take over the human will, forcing the tongue-speaker to speak. He gives the gift, but we are accountable for how it is used.

Can those who have the gift of tongues pray in this language at will? While we have no clear teaching on this in the Scripture, we do have some general principles we should consider in answering this question.

We have cases in Scripture of individuals who were gifted for a single occasion. We read the story of Balaam's donkey speaking to him in Numbers 22:28. We have no record of the donkey ever speaking again to his master. This was a one-time event which would not be repeated. God may give a gift to someone for one-time use, and this will never again be repeated. He may give a gift for a season in a person's life, and when that time is over, the gift is removed. The individuals find themselves unable to repeat what took place when they had the gift.

In other cases, the gift God gives remains with the person all their lives. Paul, for example, spoke in tongues regularly. The gift did not seem to be taken from Paul but formed a regular part of his life with the Lord. By giving him this gift, God expected Paul to use it. Writing to Timothy, the apostle would say:

[14] Do not neglect the gift you have, which was given you by prophecy when the council of elders laid their hands on you. (1 Timothy 4:14)

As with any gift, the gift of tongues can be neglected. If we have the gift, we must learn to use it properly. God gives us this language to use. We must be faithful in its use. Can a person with the gift of tongues start praying in that language whenever he or she wants? Can you pray when you want? Can you share Christ when you want? Can you exercise mercy or compassion when you want? If you want to use your gift for the Lord, He will open the door for you to use it. The same is true for the gift of tongues. If we are willing to pray or to speak in the language God gives, He will open this opportunity for us. It is His will that we use whatever gift He gives.

Is the gift given in Acts 2 different from the gift described in 1 Corinthians?

In Acts 2, specific foreign languages were spoken. 1 Corinthians 14, however, seems to speak about unknown languages. Does this mean that the gifts are different?

As a Bible teacher, I have been given by God the gift to make His Word understandable. I have accepted this gift and find great joy in using it for the glory of His name. The Lord has opened a door for the use of this gift and has provided me with small groups to teach where I live and thousands of others through the writing ministry. I have a friend who also has the gift of teaching. His gift is used as a professor in a Bible school. My wife teaches small children, something I find more difficult to do. What I am saying is that the same gift may take different forms and serve different purposes.

What is true for the gift of teaching is also true for the gift of tongues. Through this gift, God gives a language to His people. That language may be known or unknown. The gift may be used for different purposes. In Acts, it was given to confirm that God had a purpose for the Gentiles. When that purpose was made clear through the gift of tongues, God chose to use the gift for a broader purpose. It was used for praying to God, singing His praise, speaking to His people through an interpreter and for personal edification of the believer.

There is no need to see two different gifts here. It seems to me that while the gift served a different purpose, it was still a language given to His people by miraculous means.

Because this gift is so controversial, isn't it better not to encourage its use?

Some who reads this study will say: "The gift of tongues is a very controversial one in my church. To avoid controversy and division, I feel it is best not to encourage or teach on the subject."

I can understand and sympathize with where such a person. Scripture does teach that we need to be sensitive to each other and do everything for the edification of the whole body. In Romans 14, the apostle Paul reminded the Romans that not everyone would agree on what was an acceptable practice for a believer. Listen to what he says:

[5] One person esteems one day as better than another, while another esteems all days alike. Each one should be fully convinced in his own mind. [6] The one who observes the day, observes it in honour of the Lord. The one who eats, eats in honour of the Lord, since he gives thanks to God, while the one who abstains, abstains in honour of the Lord and gives thanks to God. [7] For none of us lives to himself, and none of us dies to himself. [8] For if we live, we live to the Lord, and if we die, we die to the Lord. So then, whether we live or whether we die, we are the Lord's. (Romans 14)

Paul made it clear to the Romans that it was possible for one person to observe a day for the Lord and another to abstain from that same practice for the glory of the Lord. He reminded the Romans that none of them were to live for themselves (Romans 15:7). He would go on to say:

[15] For if your brother is grieved by what you eat, you are no longer walking in love. By what you eat, do not destroy the one for whom Christ died. [16] So do not let what you regard as good be spoken of as evil. (Romans 14)

The apostle Paul encouraged those who had the freedom to eat a certain food to consider those who felt the food was unclean. It would be better not to eat that food in the presence of someone who would be offended by it. "So then let us pursue what makes for peace and mutual upbuilding," he told them in Romans 14:19. These principles apply to the use of the gift of tongues. There are churches or circumstances where it would be best to keep silent and speak only to yourself and God (see 1 Corinthians 14:28).

It is not helpful to ignore the teaching of whole sections of Scripture. This only leads to imbalance, lack of understanding and intolerance of those who practice the gift. Ignorance of Scripture is not healthy for the church. We must be willing to address what Scripture teaches and give freedom to differ in interpretation and practice. Only then can we pursue unity in the body of Christ.

I have done my best in this study to focus on the teaching of Scripture and not on personal opinion. My opinion does not carry any authority, whereas the Word of God is our authority in faith and practice. I hope that I have been faithful to the Scriptures in my interpretation of what it teaches about this gift. I trust this will help encourage greater understanding between believers of different opinions. I trust also that it will be a means of correcting any practices which are forbidden by God.

All spiritual gifts are important, and when given by God, need to be used for His glory and the edification of the body. May God be pleased to use what I have written here to bring a greater understanding of this valuable gift.

LIGHT TO MY PATH BOOK DISTRIBUTION

Light To My Path Book Distribution (LTMP) is a book writing and distribution ministry reaching out to needy Christian workers in Asia, Latin America, and Africa. Many Christian workers in developing countries do not have the resources necessary to obtain Bible training or purchase Bible study materials for their ministries and personal encouragement.

F. Wayne Mac Leod is a member of Action International Ministries and has been writing these books with a goal to distribute them freely or at cost price to needy pastors and Christian workers around the world.

These books are being used in preaching, teaching, evangelism and encouragement of local believers in over sixty countries. Books have now been translated into several languages. The goal is to make them available to as many believers as possible.

The ministry of LTMP is a faith-based ministry, and we trust the Lord for the resources necessary to distribute the books for the encouragement and strengthening of believers around the world. Would you pray that the Lord would open doors for the translation and further distribution of these books? For more information about Light To My Path Book Distribution visit our website at www.lighttomypath.ca

Printed in Great Britain
by Amazon